— DAYMOND & CO. CREATIVE

THE BRAWN OF YOUR BRAND

A BOOKLET ON AUTHENTIC PESONAL AND BUSINESS BRANDING

Begin working on your brand by starting with your mindset.

Define your brand with authenticity by honoring your truth.

DAYMOND THE BRAND, CLC

daymondcreative.com
plurapreneur.com

BRANDING IS A FORM OF EVOLUTION. EVOLVE WITH ME.

Contents

BROUGHT TO YOU BY DAYMOND & CO. & PLURAPRENEUR®

— DEDICATION

To God and the Universe.
To the Omnipotent Love and Consciousness
that works to guide us all.
Because of it, I have been nudged to write this book.
It is now complete thanks to God.

To my people, my tribe, my Evolvers . . . those I have aided on their personal journeys to brand themselves and to create the versions of themselves I loved watching bloom. Their newfound confidence and strength often warmed my heart. I was honored they believed in me enough to allow me to help shape them into who I knew they could be.

For that, I am forever thankful.

XOXO

Daymond The Brand, CLC

— ABOUT THIS BOOK

Get to Know the Power of Branding and the Part You Play in Building Your Personal and Business Brands.

The *Brawn of Your Brand* is a book developed to get readers excited about branding! Branding has become such a buzz word these days that it drums up as much confusion as it does attention. Everyone knows that branding is important. Every professional, leader, business owner, influencer, and any other person seeking to make successful strides in their fields of endeavor realize they must possess strong brands. However, branding is a very complicated activity. It is often very unsettling just figuring out exactly where to start with any branding effort, whether it's a personal branding effort or a business branding effort. Then, once that start is identified, there are a million more things to do. If we're not careful, we can easily get swept away, engaged in misguided branding efforts, incongruent with our personal desires and essence.

This book is developed to assist readers with finding a solid baseline for their difficult branding challenges. It is meant to be an enabler for readers to focus on placing their authentic selves at the center of every brand they create. This book is a breath of fresh air for its readers. It contains viewpoints about branding that encourage readers to appreciate the power of branding. It further acknowledges the ability of all readers to search inside themselves to find their own personal truths, which should be embedded in their personal and business brands. Because branding is a very difficult task, this book contains insights describing how the writer, Daymond The Brand, CLC, faced his own stressful hardships with branding. The reader will come to understand how his woes were overcome by his commitment to getting clear with himself, such that he could subsequently brand with joy. Ultimately, *The Brawn of Your Brand* is created to help readers get in touch with joyfully branding themselves and their businesses, while operating with clear intentions to experience life changing consequences.

— AUTHOR'S NOTE

The author and publisher of this work intend for this work to provide general information about the subject matter covered. This work is not intended to provide legal opinions, qualify advice, or serve as a substitute for advice by licensed, legal professionals. This work is sold with the explicit understanding that the author and the publisher of this work are not engaged in rendering legal or therapy services.

The author and publisher of this work do not warrant that this work is complete or accurate, and do not assume and hereby disclaims any liability to any person for any loss or damage caused by errors, inaccuracies or omissions, or usage of the information herein.

— PREFACE

If you purchased this book because you desire to have millions of followers, then this is not the right book for you. If you purchased this book because you want a turnkey method for establishing your brand, again, this is not the right book for you. However, if you purchased this book because you want to know how branding should work for you, contingent on you becoming very clear regarding what authentic branding is, then this is the right book for you. Additionally, you will learn how intentional branding has personally worked for me. It has brought me profound clarity and joy across several aspects of my life.

Firstly, I'd like to begin our branding journey in this book with a level set regarding why my statements on branding matter. Perhaps you want to know if my insights are based on industry facts or my own thoughts and opinions. Who am I? What validates my sentiments for branding? Those questions will undoubtedly be on your mind. So, I'll just start there.

I am Daymond The Brand, CLC. Obviously, I wasn't always so. My name is Daymond E. Lavine, and I was born in Louisiana. I am now a resident of Texas. There, I am an engineering professional as well as a business owner. I work across several industries; thus, I have evolved both in the corporate and freelance sectors. I have grown tremendously regarding my marketing design and creative expertise. That has been a paramount goal for me. Not only have I become well versed in branding and marketing myself, I have successfully done so for my clients for many years as well. I have a creative business that focuses on providing creative marketing design products and services. I further offer comprehensive brand coaching and brand consultation services for my clientele.

In recent years, I went through a rebranding effort to bring clarity and focus to my own life. I sought to create a work-life balance integral with my suite of services and businesses. As a result, Daymond & Co. was defined. My decision to emerge in the marketplace as Daymond The Brand, CLC was spawned out of that. The CLC at the end of my new name in the marketplace stands for certified life coach, as I have added coaching to my total solutions suite. Now, it should come as no surprise to you that I know a lot about branding. I work in the field. I have done it for myself, and I continue to engrain myself in it. Honestly, it was only a matter of time regarding my eventual release of this type of a book. So, here we have it: *The Brawn of Your Brand*!

For me, branding is a very important aspect of living, whether it's for personal gain or business advantages. However, my thoughts about branding go much deeper than that. Branding for me is one of my purposes for living. I know that I am supposed to be teaching it, coaching it, and consulting for it. So, that's what I do. This book is merely an extension of that purpose of mine.

What you can expect to gain from this book is a focused and personal discussion regarding branding. My attempt is to discuss branding with you in a manner you may not have experienced before. Furthermore, if you have begun participating in educating yourself in branding, thereby uncovering some of the insights I have captured herein, then I hope to concentrate those insights for you. You see, for me, I see branding as a means to package a piece of your soul for others to experience and respond to. Branding allows you to put something larger than yourself out into the world for the responses you are seeking.

As you read this book, *The Brawn of Your Brand*, I hope you gain a sense of appreciation for that title. I know how powerful both personal and business branding can be. However, it takes time and commitment to build a powerful brand. The most powerful brands have well established people with strategies working behind them. Whether a brand is built by one person or a group of people, it is still born from the DNA and souls of human beings. A brand has characteristics and presence. A brand touches people in multiple ways, depending on what it was created to do. *A brand has life!* And when you read this book, you will learn how to begin viewing your brand as the powerful entity it was meant to be. That's my desire for you as you turn the pages of this book.

I've been helping people improve their lives and businesses through fantastic branding efforts and tactical branding practices for years. However, I do most of that work on a one-on-one basis. Performing my work that way has been very intentional. I commit to my clients and dive deep into the activities we want to accomplish together. However, I have been recently nudged by the Universe to extend my reach. I now seek to empower people with enlightening branding thoughts and insights beyond my current region and immediate sphere of influence. It is impossible for me to reach everyone who could possibly benefit from the insights and advice I have to offer. However, this book is now created to help me remedy that situation, to some extent. When you read this book, I hope you feel as if you are chatting directly with me. Along the way, please allow me to help you brand yourself with your heart, your mind, and your soul fully engaged.

Now, let's begin.

— I. YOUR BRAND IS YOUR BADGE OF HONOR.

The Highlights of This Section You Should Know:

- ***You will understand your branding efforts can be based on your own personal truth to represent your best interest and your heart's desires.***

- ***You will learn from my powerful insights regarding how I was forced to engage in intentional branding because of my past disappointing outcomes.***

- ***You will begin to perceive your brand as a badge of honor to be polished over time for added value to your life and your business efforts.***

Today, everyone knows that a brand can make or break a business. It can also make or break a person. Here and now, in the early twenty-first century, competition in the marketplace at all levels–community-based, across the states, across the nation, and even globally–is extremely treacherous. Businesses are continually vying for top rankings to score the most clientele, supporters, and revenues in all fields of commerce. Industry leaders, influencers, and social disruptors are doing all they can to be seen and heard above all else so their agendas may take flight. Through branding efforts—albeit the strategies, messaging, product attributes, service attributes, and consumer confidence that gets engrained throughout all of them—businesses and people endlessly contribute to shifting thoughts and responses of the masses. Thus, marketplace trends and predictions remain an ever changing target to hit. Everyone continues to try to understand them for the sake of revenue generation. Although people may never truly understand trending outcomes for sure-footed success in both life and business, everyone undoubtedly knows that branding is a huge contributor to being successful.

People and businesses that have become very accustomed to branding seem to always know what to do in the crazy world of commerce as the social and economic climates change. There are many that seem to always know how to persevere through the many changes that come along. It's as if nothing can harm them. To the average onlooker, that's what it appears to be: big brands stay big and win big, no matter what. Thus, only if you're directly involved in the day to day affairs of those people and businesses with super solid brands in place, do you know what it truly takes to sustain their business affairs. Still, there is one thing that can be said for them for sure: these people and businesses truly know *their brands have brawn*!

A brand is like a badge of honor. Your brand is an expression of the pride you take in doing whatever it is that you do. And in most cases, the strength of your brand is directly proportional to the amount of work you do to build it. I'd like to pause here and have you pause as well because it's important that you fully absorb this fact. We as human beings have a natural inclination to spend a lot of time doing what comes naturally for us, whether that is for our betterment or detriment. So that means, if we're not careful, we might spend most of our time doing things we love to do, although those things do not improve our lives, nor highlight the best versions of ourselves. In this very specific case, as it relates to personal or business branding, what occurs is that a person may brand themself or their business in a haphazard manner. If this happens, they will surely end up creating brands for themselves that they haven't even prepared for. Because they didn't intentionally set out to align their activities with their lives and their business goals, they will cause people to perceive them in unknown ways. These perceptions will often catch them off guard and unprepared to acknowledge. This occurrence plays out in simple, recurrent ways that either make or break us. We may not even realize that we've poorly branded ourselves and our businesses in the minds of other people who take us at our face value . . . literally. We may not know it, and we may not like it.

I personally underwent unintentional personal branding at one point in my life. I went through disappointment and surprise. I wondered what I had done and how much I had done to convince people that I had characteristics and traits I was unaware of. I became harshly critical of myself as a result, and I remember how horrible I felt. I was so hard on myself back then. What benefitted me in that situation however was my resilience and commitment to tapping into the spiritual connection I developed with my inner self, the Universe, and God. In my moments of bitter self-loathing and despair, I retreated into my thoughts. I sought out inspiration whether I found it in the media, books, people I knew, or just the simple happiness I created from thankfulness despite my shortcomings. I sought out my awakening. I desired to uncover how the perception of others in my professional and social circles either helped or hindered me from creating the future I wanted for myself. Then, one day, it just came to me: "If you don't think you have a personal brand, I'm here to tell you that you do. And if you're not controlling it, then someone else is." That's what the voice inside my head revealed to me. As I pondered that revelation and yielded to God's intention for me, I realized that I had finally found the remedy for transforming my disappointment into joy.

As you may already know, I've operated in the space of graphic design since the mid 1990s. In my high school years, I assisted our athletics department and yearbook team with graphic design work and other visually creative content. As I continued my education in college in the fields of physics and electrical engineering, I freelanced by producing flyers for parties and events to keep extra cash in my pockets. After graduating from college, and landing my engineering job in Texas, I still maintained my side-hustle by starting a graphic design business. My skills sharpened as I helped many of my clients with their marketing design efforts for their business needs. Most of my clients were and still are budding entrepreneurs seeking to build their images in their respective fields. Thus, before the infinite world of branding grew to become the monstrous beast that everyone is aware of today (but few knew how to tame), I had already been "branding" my clients. Early on, I didn't call it branding however. Instead, I referred to it as *marketing design consistency*. It was branding nonetheless, and I mention this background of mine because it was pivotal in the application of a skill I already had to better myself for who I am today.

Years ago, I was searching for answers regarding what I should do and who I should be. Luckily, it was revealed to me that I already knew what to do to create a new version of me, one that I would know better and love more. I knew that I needed to offer that new version of myself to the world. I just needed to work at it. If I did, then that version of me would be more intentional and more purposeful. Furthermore, if I fully developed it through personal branding, thereby announcing to the world who I am, what I stand for, what I do, how I do it, and why I do it, then I knew that I would finally be happy. I knew that once I controlled the narrative for myself exuding the characteristics, messaging, and imagery that blended my life and my life's work deliberately and unapologetically, then I would lovingly own that. Every action I would perform combined with the responsiveness I would receive would be exactly as it should be. Most importantly, I would be me, *authentically me.* That would be my brand. So now, everything I do has a little piece of my deliberate, personal branding pulled right into it.

Is living your brand in truth a desire for you? Are you looking to understand what branding is, what it should mean for you, and what it can do for you? Perhaps you're looking to see beyond the surface level insights you already know about branding. Did you purchase my book because you believe you will learn something different from what you already know? Maybe you will; maybe you won't. But I can guarantee you will receive my personal insights regarding how you can brand yourself in accordance with your unique reason for being. After all these years of working with my branding clients, what I have come to learn is that everyone thinks they have a great handle on their branding, or at least a handle that is good enough. And for those things they don't know about branding, they push them aside believing all will be okay. But is just okay acceptable for you? Or do you want something better? I have been able to witness firsthand the inconsistency between who people want to be and what they want their businesses to be, versus what their personal brands and business brands actually represent. I have also observed their reservations regarding pushing their branding efforts to the next level. I know for a fact that many people are fine with limping along in their branding efforts in both life and business, just because it's easier. It's easier to do that than come to terms with making uncomfortable adjustments in their lives. The truth is that many people are afraid to grow. They know that growth is difficult. They're afraid of doing what it takes to rise to new expectations and ways of maneuvering in life, even though those changes are ones they will make for the better. When you're ready, you will know it, just like I did. If you purchased my book to reveal some depth in branding you may never have read before, then you will get that. For me, branding is more than just a set of actions and steps people take to market themselves and their businesses. It's also a mental and soulful journey that

"THE TRUTH IS THAT MANY PEOPLE ARE AFRAID TO GROW. THEY'RE AFRAID OF DOING WHAT IT TAKES TO RISE TO NEW EXPECTATIONS AND WAYS OF MANEUVERING IN LIFE, EVEN THOUGH THOSE CHANGES ARE ONES THEY WILL MAKE FOR THE BETTER."

weaves your purpose into the fabric of what you do and how the world responds to you as a result. I love working with my clients on a one-on-one basis to create these breakthroughs for themselves. Now, through this book, I'm extending my reach to you. I hope you enjoy it.

How did the lack of intentional personal branding affect me?

Regardless of whether or not you have been intentional with your brand, your brand will most certainly land you wherever you should be in life at any given moment. It's all dependent on just how much time and attention you devote to it. How you are perceived and where you land in life is all dependent on you, and your personal brand is a part of that. This was something I learned the hard way in my corporate career as opportunities came my way. I've always been a problem solver, so it makes perfect sense that I am an engineer. As I racked up the years in my corporate profession, getting known as a great team member, capable of independence, little need for direction, and the ability to solve tough problems on teams in the systems engineering environment, I noticed over time that I would get deployed to efforts that exhausted a lot of my time and energy. My leadership loved it. For them, I had become someone who could step into chaotic situations, and fix the critical issues at hand. So, as I worked on various efforts, thereby improving my leadership skills and technical abilities, I became mentality drained and physically affected by all of the stress that compiled on me over the many years. I was forced to try to figure out what was going on with me because I became very unhappy, even as I moved up the ranks. I was emotionally drained. Even worse, there came a point whereas every time I entered the office, headaches would ensue. My physical state of being was suffering because I had gotten myself into roles at work that weakened my physical health. I even endured the onset of a sight-debilitating condition called central serous retinopathy. It's a disorder that causes the accumulation of fluid under the macula in one eye. That eye would otherwise be healthy; however, the fluid causes blurring of the vision in the eye. I had to do something about this. I had to do more than go to the doctor and seek treatment for my eye. I had to do more than find time to exercise and release my stress at the gym. I had to figure out what was the root cause of me allowing my livelihood to be chipped away by exhaustion and stress.

I was consumed with being the "the problem solver." Regardless of how chaotic a work environment had become, or how complicated achieving success seemed to be, I was known as a hard worker who could enter a program area or join a team, and save the day. That was it. That's what I had established myself to be. I had branded myself as "Daymond The Problem Solver for Broken Issues." After spending late hours at night before my slumber trying to figure out what was happening to me, the answer came. I was not controlling whom I was becoming in my business environment. I was not commanding people's perceptions of me based on what I wanted people to see me as. I was not building and sustaining a personal brand for myself at work that I was happy with. Because of that, I was haphazardly allowing myself to be put into chaotic work environments, instead of seeking out the opportunities I preferred to thrive in.

I decided to take matters into my own hands instead of letting others figure out where they wanted me to be or what they wanted from me. I began to think about how I would approach my leadership using deliberate language to convey what I wanted out of my career. When I approached them, I mentioned my disappointment in the roles I was receiving, even though I was rewarded with monetary incentives and promotions. When I was countered with the fact that leadership thought I was doing a great job persevering in stressful environments, I mentioned that this recognition was actually counterproductive to my optimal performance as a satisfied employee. Instead of always solving problems other people created, I figured it was time for me to be on the front end of new starts and projects beginning to roll out at the company. That way, I could influence change and predictively circumvent issues on the horizon, similar to those I had already experienced in the past. Honestly, I wanted to be in the position to solve my own problems. This was my attempt to pivot my brand, reduce my stress, and increase my happiness with work. And I was determined to stick to it as firmly as I could because, for the first time in my life, I was branding myself in accordance with my truth and my needs. Needless to say, presently I am happy with where I am in my career and with the roles I have been able to attain in my engineering environment. I began to express a personal brand that captured my dedication, determination, and ability to lead and start things, with independence and careful attention to strategic methodologies.

From that point forward, after personally applying personal branding to my life, and learning just how important and powerful personal branding is, I decided to make a commitment to both myself and my clients to do more. That was the reason for the derivation of my personal branding training class called **Personal Branding 101**. After getting my life coaching certification in 2019, I also decided to add

Branding on Purpose as one of my coaching focuses. I must also say that my experience with personal branding throughout my corporate environment continues. I still use personal branding to gain the outcomes I desire throughout many of my activities that I participate in to this very day.

Years ago, I had another situation where I was faced with opening a brick and mortar space in association with my entrepreneurial activities. I pondered back and forth: would this space be my office space for business relations or something else? As I thought about it more and more, and looked around the space to figure out how it might fit into my life and my efforts, ideas began to bud. While those ideas grew in my mind, I knew from the very start that the space would need to fit into my life, what I was doing, and what I wanted to come next for myself. I was learning how to extend my personal brand into my business affairs, both from a corporate and a freelance perspective. Thus, I knew this space would need to be a part of my personal branding activities. I wrote my desires down. I captured the fact that the space needed to mirror something that I was already working well in my life. That something was my graphic design and branding business, so I decided to make the space an event venue and an extension of my creativity. My thought was that as it would generate funds, it would also strengthen the creative side of me. I decorated the space, and I prepared it for receiving business. I worked very hard to have my new space embody the very words I put into my business plan. I further intentionally applied some of my personal and my business branding elements to the decor as well as the marketing materials for the space. After that, I solicited feedback. When customers and clients walked in, they described how much they liked the space and what it felt like to them. Amazingly, they literally repeated words directly back to me that I already put in my plan. They had no idea they were doing so. So, yes! I know just how powerful branding can be! And when you're intentional, deliberate, and authentic with your branding, whether it's personal or business related, you will see that you will get the results that you desire.

Looking over my past, I now see that precise intentions are the winds that power my sails for exceptional branding that is congruent with my life goals. I offer the understanding of this same clarity to you, so that you too can enhance your life. My objective is to help you understand branding in a brand new way. It's something I work with people on to integrate into their creative marketing and branding efforts. It's something I also provide to my brand coaching clients who desire the integration of purposeful branding with their personal and business branding activities. The main point I'm making here is that you cannot "brand on purpose" if you do not know your intentions for branding. In essence, the lack of intentional branding will almost certainly lead you down a path in life you will not like. Perhaps you're already traveling that path, disappointed with your outcomes, and not quite sure how to fix the problem and where to start with the fix. If you haven't been intentional regarding your personal and business branding activities, then think about some of your current results. Are they undesirable because you haven't been clear with yourself? If so, then that is the reason for you reading my words now. I challenge you to clear your mind and be flexible as you read on. I also urge you to be honest with yourself. Could you be doing more to take your brand into your own hands and create something you love? Is the problem that you do not know where to start? If so, my most basic answer to you is

"LOOKING OVER MY PAST, I NOW SEE THAT PRECISE INTENTIONS ARE THE WINDS THAT POWER MY SAILS FOR EXCEPTIONAL BRANDING THAT IS CONGRUENT WITH MY LIFE GOALS."

start wherever you feel you can. Do not delay. Every second of every day is another moment to take matters into your own hands. Yes, I know branding is a huge effort to confront. So, as you read on, perhaps pull out some of the questions I ask to you throughout this book. Answer those questions. If your answers are vague, then start by getting clear with those. Then, work to perform actions in association with the clarity you will surely gain.

Let me repeat it: your brand is your badge of honor.

Like all nice badges, your brand will eventually begin to lose its luster. It will fade and become worn due to time. Depending on how much you "wear it" and put it to good use, your brand will become old, no longer capturing the attention of new onlookers as it had during its novelty. However, there are things you can do to ensure your honor never fades. In fact, I actually think it's okay that your brand grows old. But it will either grow old and die, or grow old and formidable. Obviously, you desire the latter. And there is an easy way I can help put this into perspective by drawing a parallel between branding and building a family.

As you enter into adulthood, and you begin to know all of your wonderful qualities, and the not so great ones as well, you will desire to instill all those good traits in your children. You will notice them and reward your children for exuding those good traits. You will talk to your children and guide them to do more of those good things, and even improve them. For the not so great traits your children inherit from you, you will attempt to chastise them for those. You might even try to stir them away from demonstrating those bad behaviors altogether. In essence, you'll strive to make sure your children don't make the same mistakes you made growing up.

Those good traits you admire in yourself that you heartily desire to pass on to your children are somewhat like a brand. They are characteristics that people have come to know you and your children for. They might even be a source of pride for you and your family. They will be familial qualities that your family is known for. Community members might look up to your family just because of them. So, think about how that came to be. Your children are an extension of you, and the characteristics that you will have instilled in them will be more polished and refined because of you. You will have worked at it. That was your intention. And there you have it! Your family's honor and legacy will continue. That is how you will do your part to ensure your family's brand is continually polished and refined as time goes on.

If you don't have any children, like me, it's okay. Please allow me to call upon another analogous situation regarding your brand being a badge of honor you must polish over time. Think about how you might start a business and apply a brand design to it. You'll think of the business name and ensure it has a nice ring to it when it's said aloud. You'll think of a logo and color scheme to go along with your brand for your business. You'll think of a tagline, hashtags, and an elevator pitch perhaps. All of this would be captured in the brand guide for your business. Your color swatch will be seen countless times. Your hashtags will be used time and time again. You'll say your elevator pitch so much that you'll become sick of repeating it. And your responses from the overall market place will eventually taper off. But if you have been a good steward of your business brand while running your business, you will have been taking note of the portions of your branding strategy that performed well while others did not. You will have worked to improve or retire bad branding practices while refining or even evolving the great branding practices that were already in place. In essence you will have been polishing your branding badge of honor. You will have been ensuring that although your business brand was becoming old news, what it stands for was becoming as precious as gold.

Is powerful, long lasting branding something you desire for yourself or your business? Do you want to be known for something that withstands the test of time? Do you want people to know about your business while having wonderful thoughts automatically pop into their minds? Do you want to enforce those good thoughts with positive outcomes for your business? Well, as you read on, I hope you come to realize that branding is not only great for both yourself and your business; branding is also priceless. Literally, you cannot price a solid, well-known brand because you cannot put a price tag on people's perceptions which yield countless successful outcomes. That simply just cannot be quantified in totality.

What should you do after reading this section?

1. *Determine the most important personal truth you would like to reveal to the world through your unique branding efforts.*

2. *Define what you think branding means in general versus what you would like it to mean for you.*

3. *Define what you consider to be the most difficult aspects of branding for you to address. Try to decide what you will do to overcome your branding blockers.*

— II. YOUR BRAND IS A WONDERFUL FRIEND.

The Highlights of This Section You Should Know:

- ***You will gain the perspective of appreciating your brand as your confidence-boosting best friend. You will learn that your personal brand or business brand protects you in the marketplace.***

- ***You will come to realize the essence of your brand comes from you. Yet, your brand can exist completely outside of you. It is another life changing entity that works with you and for you.***

- ***You will understand that if you are clear and honest when developing your brand, then it will emerge with clarity and honesty for you and your onlookers. If you are dishonest and messy while developing your brand, then it will emerge reflecting dishonesty and messiness for you and your onlookers.***

- ***You will further begin to think of branding as something easier accomplished if it is grounded in truth and authenticity.***

I love when I sometimes tell my branding clients, "Your brand is like your best friend." Everytime I say it, it excites me because it's empowering. There are so many places to turn to and look for answers outside ourselves, especially today. But a brand, if developed authentically, comes from within. Everytime we look at someone else, or some news channel, or some television show to instruct us regarding how we should act or do or be, we relinquish a little more of our power to guide our own souls. Inherently, we most often know what's right for us. But society makes it so easy for us to allow ourselves to become brainwashed, while we brush off just how uniquely gifted we all are. What's so beautiful about branding is that it allows you to package all of your good stuff: your thoughts, your ideas, your principles, the fantastic things you do, and the wonderful ways you do them. When you're all done, it's as if you've created a new person or entity. This new being is capable of working with you to do things in your life that enhance your path forward, whether that involves creating the life you desire or running a business congruent with your entrepreneurial goals. However, your brand can only do this for you if you invest in building that relationship in truth and honesty. You must take solitary moments to sit with yourself and think about what you desire. Then, you must create the embodiment of that based on your own internal needs and desires. If you do this, over time, you will discover something amazing. Either a new version of you will emerge, your personal brand, or a new extension of you will emerge, a well-defined and well-branded business.

> **"THE CREATION OF A NEW BRAND IS PHENOMENAL. WHAT ELSE COULD DESCRIBE THE CREATION OF SOMETHING THAT NEVER EXISTED BEFORE, SOMETHING THAT BECOMES A LIVING THING THAT CAN CHANGE LIVES?"**

The creation of a new brand is phenomenal. There is no other word for it. What else could describe the creation of something that never existed before, something that becomes a living thing that can change lives? That's what a brand does. It can live beyond the thoughts that initially contrived it and beyond the plans that were first put in place for it. Still, a brand cannot exist on its own. It needs people. A brand requires the exertion of strength and energy. That power must come from people. If *you* are building a brand, then that power must come from *you*. You must breathe life into your brand whether it is your own personal brand or one for a business you own. The more you pour into your brand makes for the better it will be. It will grow to be a healthy companion for you. It will also thrive and thus possess the ability to pour back into you. If you are truly intentional and committed to building your brand, it will support you in ways that will eventually fill in the gaps for things you ordinarily don't have strength or confidence to accomplish. It might even surprise you with accomplishments you never expected. Your brand will become *your best friend*.

"BEING CLEAR AND REAL WITH YOURSELF PRIOR TO AND WHILE BUILDING YOUR BRAND OPENS THE APERTURE FOR AUTHENTICITY."

So, how exactly do you seek out this new friend of yours? I can tell you it won't be easy. But aren't all friendships difficult at some point along the way? As is the case with building friendships, developing a brand requires understanding and transparency. Both of these requirements are equally challenging to maintain over extended periods of time. And just as the case for building friendships requires careful thought as to whether you are in it for the long haul or the short run, you must absolutely consider this for your personal or business brand. Hopefully, you want your brand to live a long and fruitful life, yielding lots of prosperity as the fruits of your initial toils and thoughtfulness. But in order for that to happen, your hard work should include you being clear and upfront with not only what you want from your brand, but also what you bring to it. After all, compatibility is a factor that matters for any relationship. Reciprocity ensures the relationship endures whatever hardships may come along. Your brand is no exception.

One of the most difficult challenges you'll face with creating your new brand, i.e. developing your new companion, will be being transparent and truthful with yourself. You must be real with yourself and see reality for what it is before you build a relationship with something else based upon your perceived truth. There are things about you that are great, and there are others that are not. Branding yourself or your business must consider these characteristics of yours. Those characteristics should be unfiltered and forthcoming.

The fact is, most of us are often very delusional with ourselves at times because we choose to see ourselves in ways that make us feel superficially happy. We typically just want to zone in on those characteristics of ours that make us feel great about who we are and what we do. We all think we're awesome, right? It's great to have confidence, but what is the benefit of lying to ourselves, especially when we are seeking to improve ourselves and find our joyful truths? Yes, you might falsely frame your life and existence in a cute little bubble of beauty and colorful perfection. However, that bubble will eventually pop one day, only to leave you surprised or maybe even sad. Let me give you some advice. It's just better that you pop that bubble for yourself in the very beginning, instead of leaving it up to chance to unexpectantly do that for you.

Being clear and real with yourself prior to and while building your brand opens the aperture for authenticity. Who doesn't want that in a relationship? And as with all budding relationships, authenticity is better experienced in the beginning of a relationship rather than somewhere later down the road, out of the blue. Think about the many relationships you have with people, your friends, your family, your children, or even your romantic interests. Have you had friends, family, or lovers disappoint you because they revealed to you their true actions, motives, or thoughts of betrayal, unexpectedly? Have you tried to raise your children well only to have them sometimes do things like lie to you, leave you in the dark, and get themselves into trouble? Then, in your state of disappointment, were you forced to come to their aid? Your brand will have a relationship with you that operates in a similar fashion. The main difference however is that you have full control of it, what it does for you, and how you will, in turn, respond to it. Because of this, your brand will reflect back to you exactly what you gave it. Yes, your brand will uphold its end of the bargain each and every time. It will reciprocate whatever it is that you offer. If you are truthful with it, it will be truthful with you. If you are fake with it, it will be fake with you. Lie to it, and it will lie back. If you are intentional and deliberate with your brand, then it will be intentional and deliberate with you. And here is something extremely important for you to remember: everything your brand reflects back at you will be on display for all those you interact with to see, observe, and respond to as well.

When you are authentic, it is undeniable. People can see it and feel it. I have been working with people branding themselves and their businesses for a long time. I know what it looks like to see them unlock new experiences in life and business while they develop and grow. I can also feel the happiness they feel when they know they're on the right track with branding. That's what I help them accomplish. In doing so, I directly witness them reaping the benefits of intertwining their truths with their personal and business brands. That is what they learn from our working together. And just as I am urging you to live your truth as a part of creating your brand in this book, so do I. I live in my own personal truth while my personal brand and business brands reflect exactly that.

I have been told by others that they see the comfort, confidence, and ease I exude throughout my branding efforts. When provided the opportunity, I say back to them, "It is hard work, but I'm real. What you see is my brand. You see the packaging of who I am to show you what's needed when it's needed." Some of that confidence and ease is grounded in my background. As an only child from a small city, I have always been very comfortable existing in my own space, doing my own thing, with very few people around me. Yes, I am an introvert. However, when I fully accepted this truth about myself, I quickly learned I was holding myself back from fulfilling my purpose of helping, coaching, and inspiring others. Had I remained hindered by the desire to stay secluded and distant from others, then I would now be unfulfilled. I know that for sure. I needed something to help get me out of my own way. Can you see now that my brand has become my best friend? It has allowed me to do so much more and be so much more than I once thought I could be. It has allowed me to be more present for you. It has indeed enabled me to write this book for you.

Trust me, you will see. Continue to read on. Continue to learn how branding can become easier for you. As you read my book, my aspiration for you is that you become even more of who you are meant to be. It is my hope for you that you not only learn how powerful you can become through branding, but also know that you can tap into so much more of your potential. Your brand will be a friend that takes every step along the way with you. I'm here to guide you to that.

What should you do after reading this section?

1. *Converse with your brand as if it is a new friend you are honoring and acknowledging. Ask it what it is and how it views itself today. Dig deeper and question what it desires to be in the future.*

2. *Determine your new commitments for building your personal or business brand based on what you believe you want it to be. Remember, your brand has told you what it desires to be as well. Figure out how you will blend those desires.*

— III. YOU SHOULD KNOW WHAT OTHERS KNOW ABOUT YOU.

The Highlights of This Section You Should Know:

- *You will realize that branding helps level set everyone who comes to know you or your business. Everyone is always trying to figure out everyone else. Branding facilitates that understanding.*

- *You will take note that branding can be a primary contributor to you reaching or failing to reach your goals in life and business. People and opportunities will show up for you based on your branding practices.*

- *You will understand that self awareness should be embedded in your branding practices. Your characteristics are embedded in your branding efforts; thus, you want to manage how well your*

characteristics align with you reaching your personal and business goals.

- ***You will be encouraged to refrain from inauthentic branding. Inauthentic branding is like false advertisement. It eventually reveals itself, and the fallout is difficult to overcome.***

Everyone has their own ideas and assumptions about you. No matter what you do or no matter where you go, this will always be the case for you. Yes, I get it, no one wants to be judged. However, let's face the facts. You are always on trial. Everyone is always trying to figure out everyone else. Figuring people out is how we learn to align ourselves with others. This is a natural part of life. As a matter of fact, there are people you are trying to figure out and whom you think you have figured out at this very moment as well. You probably can name a couple of people you call friends because of the ideals and principles they offer. They seem like great acquaintances you should have in your life. Additionally, there are some people you are absolutely steadfast on never

> **"YOU ARE ALWAYS ON TRIAL. EVERYONE IS ALWAYS TRYING TO FIGURE OUT EVERYONE ELSE."**

getting to know at all. There may be others whom you have at one time thought you wanted to have around as friends, but after some time and consideration, your assessment of the relationship caused you to pull away. This doesn't only happen with people, it happens with businesses and companies we support in our lives too. There are products and services we buy because we like what they are and how the company markets them. There are some companies we buy products and services from because we like what those companies offer and stand for. Some of those companies may be wonderful to their employees. Some may make you, as a consumer, feel special. Some might perform noble efforts to address environmental concerns. Either you have people in your life or you support businesses and purchase from them because of the many things you know about them. And believe it or not, people have you in their lives or businesses cater to you because of what they know about you too.

So, as it relates to branding, what do you know about yourself? Again, if you don't think you have a brand, I'm here to tell you that you do. And if you cannot answer the question, that means you have a brand now that you are not in control of. What I mean by this is that you are a part of the world, and the world is responding to you based on how you operate in it at this very moment. There are ideals you currently represent and stand for. You are subconsciously sticking with them and asserting them for everyone else around you. At the same time, you have goals and aspirations. There are some things you want to accomplish with your life or your business, and they potentially may or may not be aligned with what you're putting out into the world. You may not be doing enough to reach your goals. You may even be the root cause of your inability to achieve some wins in life. The cause, you ask? Well, your ineffective or mismanaged branding is sending out the wrong messages. Isn't that a powerful thought to process?

If your branding is ineffective or mismanaged, people will notice that about you. Their commentary may come out in ways you would never have imagined. Have you done something you considered to be a big deal in your life or a major accomplishment, and when you shared this with people, they didn't think it was very serious? Have you heard about people saying things about you from secondhand sources that weren't true or were out of character for you because they misconstrued some actions you made? Perhaps they misinterpreted some statements you offered? Have you been ridiculed for an outfit you wore in an environment where it was inappropriate? Has someone treated you a certain way or made an assumption about you simply because of the way you looked? Have you marketed a business of yours, and certain types of clientele you were attempting to tap into would not respond?

"IF YOUR BRANDING IS INEFFECTIVE OR MISMANAGED, PEOPLE WILL NOTICE THAT ABOUT YOU."

Believe it or not, the undesirable responses you received from people or the marketplace were symptoms of you not paying careful attention to the components of your branding. Those components were thus interpreted out of alignment or out of context with your desires. In the case of someone or people not taking your endeavors seriously, the issue could be that you had not taken time out for yourself to put a branding practice in place. You must baseline your social activities and level set people for what's new and exciting in your life. In order for people to take you seriously, you must first take yourself seriously. You must share with people and the marketplace what and why you are doing what you are doing. The clearer you are will make for the more confidence you will gain in sharing things about yourself and marketing yourself or your business. And when people see your confidence, they will be more likely to believe in you and the message you are coupling with your confidence. Your personal brand or business brand will help you with your confidence. Just as a best friend would do, your brand will pump you up in the moments you need it most.

However, just because you have confidence, that doesn't mean you are genuine. And if you are not genuine, this will ooze through your branding efforts. There are lots of people and brands that are confident about who and what they have defined themselves to be. But fake brands and fake people usually burn bright, then burn out. They sometimes leave a wake of destruction and collateral damage behind. Eventually, fake personal brands and business brands must be reinvented. Reinvention for fake brands usually means coming to terms with the falsehoods they have been putting out, only to fade into obscurity or shine in re-emergence. We often see this play out in the media and marketplace. For the

"IN ORDER FOR PEOPLE TO TAKE YOU SERIOUSLY, YOU MUST FIRST TAKE YOURSELF SERIOUSLY."

sake of keeping this book legally sound, I will not name any famous people you may have read about on gossip websites or seen on talk shows. But let me just say here that the lucrative field of public relations exists exactly because of this. Some of our favorite television shows point this fact out. Think about *Scandal* with Olivia Pope and *Flack* with Anna Paquin.

Also, let's not fool ourselves; image is everything. How we and our businesses appear to others matters, no matter how much we try to avoid it. You will hear me say this and see me post about it from time to time. I often provide guidance to my followers and clients through messaging around "being yourself" and "being authentic" as they grow and evolve their brands. Some might argue, "Well, how can I be myself if I have an image I must portray throughout my branding efforts?" I say to people, "You already have an image, and that image should simply be refined, not changed, to highlight what you want your branding practices to do for you." Keeping with the analogy that your brand is like your best friend, your brand (business or personal) should allow for some particulars that keep you well informed as to whether or not you are making good decisions. When you say something wrong, or wear the wrong thing, or put the wrong imagery out in the market, your brand should nudge you on the shoulder and say, "Hey, something's not right here." When you put imagery and content out there that doesn't align with the mission and purposes of your business, again, your brand should say, "Hold up, I think something is not fitting with the original plan and vision we developed." Most importantly, your branding will reveal to others whether or not you are authentic. It will even show to others that you are deceptive, if indeed that is the case. That's because you or your business will need to perform actions that go hand in hand with how you present, or market, yourself or your business. Marketing is the practice of aligning your operations with your branding efforts. It's at the core of the fact that you can't only *show* when it comes to branding. You must *show and prove.*

Many people face the consequences of branding themselves in manners that are false or inauthentic. We see this scenario play out very often. We may either witness someone rise and fall because their actions are unable to keep up with the stories they have spun about themselves. They may have obtained various opportunities or become a part of some social circles only to let down those who depended on them. It frequently happens as people get to know one another either through business affiliations or social courtships. It may have even happened to you. I know there have been moments in my life when I created narratives about myself so that I would be accepted by others. These narratives became components of the personal brand I was attempting to create so that I could associate with others. You may be able to think of moments like this for yourself. Ultimately, what happens is that the inauthenticity becomes overbearing. For me, it added additional stresses to my life that were not worth me sacrificing my genuine nature. I found myself always trying to prove myself worthy of having social connections I was forcing to exist. I would perform actions that were typically out of the ordinary for me and incongruent with who I was at the core. Remember, I'm an introvert. In addition to that, I also observed the fact that because the connections I was establishing were forced, the people I was trying to connect with did not respond to me as I expected. There were questions about my intentions or validity in being a part of their circles. There were even questions I had for myself such as "Is this forced connection really worth the gain . . . or lack thereof?" and "Does this extra pressure I'm putting on myself align with my God-given purposes?" I suspect you have had similar situations happen

"MANY PEOPLE FACE THE CONSEQUENCES OF BRANDING THEMSELVES IN MANNERS THAT ARE FALSE OR INAUTHENTIC."

in your life. In those moments, your greatest lesson learned should be your awareness of you not operating in authenticity. You were not operating in a manner that resonated with your reason for being. Instead, you simply wanted to do something or be someone that seemed appealing to you for all the wrong reasons. You may have admired how people looked or interacted in a certain social group. You may have liked what people seemed to have accomplished or admired the assets they attained. You may have liked the way they dressed. You may have liked the businesses or companies they operate or thrive in. But did you really take time out to think about how the things in their lives align with the things in yours? One of the hardest lessons we'll ever learn in life is to not compare ourselves to others. It's at the heart of exactly why I have written this book for you. Find your purpose. Build your brand. Live your life. *Be that.*

"FIND YOUR PURPOSE. BUILD YOUR BRAND. LIVE YOUR LIFE. BE THAT."

#BeYourBestYOU.

What should you do after reading this section?

1. ***Think about how you or your business exist in the world today. Then, identify whether or not it is being mismanaged by you. Identify the areas of mismanagement you would like to improve for your branding efforts.***

2. ***If you have begun focusing on your branding efforts already, identify the sources for those efforts. Identify which ones of those sources align with you versus what you are mimicking of other people or businesses.***

3. ***If you are branding yourself or your business already, then identify what is working well for you versus what is not. Map all of your activities to your genuine efforts versus those that are inauthentic, or mimicked. Perform an assessment***

for yourself to uncover your branding trend.

4. *Identify the changes you would like to apply to your current branding efforts, based on item #3 above.*

— IV. PACKAGE YOUR BRAND BY BEING SPIRITUAL WITH IT.

The Highlights of This Section You Should Know:

- ***You will realize branding creates a contrived perception that is best consumed by the general marketplace if it is well presented. Still, your truth can be and should be embedded in your branding efforts.***

- ***You will understand that branding is highly susceptible to criticism. You will be challenged to sift through all the feedback to find your voice. A recommendation is for you to respond to your voice first.***

- ***You will gain powerful insights from me regarding why it's best to embed your soul into your personal and business branding efforts. I believe branding can be spiritual.***

For some reason, many people believe that having confidence about themselves equates to caring nothing about what other people think about them. Nothing could be further from the truth. I hope that everyone who reads this book recognizes not only the power of branding, but also realizes imagery is a primary and fundamental component of it. This is exactly why every large company considers their branding an essential part of their intellectual property. They own the imagery and message for what enables their success. Branding is directly utilized on a daily basis to ensure sales and consumer support meet mission goals and business plans. We should learn from these large companies. Whether we are personally branding ourselves or our small businesses, we should take our branding efforts just as seriously as those large companies do. Today, nearly every consumer directly or indirectly knows what a strong and cohesive brand looks like. Not everyone can articulate it, but most people know a great brand when they see one. That's all because companies have trained us over the decades to recognize solid branding. Today, they are quite splendid at it.

Branding is the activity of packaging a perception. When I mention this, I not only mean how you perceive yourself or your company, but also how others perceive you or your company. Often, a huge gap exists between the internal views we hold and the perceived views of others regarding those same things we see and experience together. For this exact reason, you should care about what others think. You should not care because you want to absorb their views and compromise your intrinsic values. You should not use anyone else's views to convert yourself into someone you are not or convert your company to one that does not resonate with your unique purposes in life. Instead, you should use the perceptions of others for exactly what they are, external data. The beauty of this mindset is that when you see the views of others as external data, then you get to do with that data exactly what you want to do with it. Thus, if your desire is to level up your personal brand or your business brand so that you get the results you desire, then you do your own assessment of the

"BRANDING IS THE ACTIVITY OF PACKAGING A PERCEPTION."

data. Filter out what you need from your assessment of those external views, and use that to your advantage, exactly as *you* see fit.

When you go into the mental space of assessing the views of others for your own benefit, it becomes vital for you to keep in mind you being kind, fair, and objective with yourself. It's in our human nature to only want the best for ourselves. So, we often couple wanting the best for ourselves with always wanting to view ourselves in a positive way. We tend to react to the feedback we receive about ourselves or our businesses in a defensive manner. By doing so, however, we stunt our ability to grow and become better. In addition to that, we sometimes not only allow the feedback of others to put us in a state of defensiveness; we also do it to ourselves by being too hard on ourselves. We might tailspin into a mental space of defensiveness along with sadness and anger. I've actually been guilty of this. So, you may be wondering, "Well, if I should care about what others think regarding my business or my personal brand, then how do I do that without taking it personally? How do I just treat that feedback as data that I need to improve my brand?" I have an answer for you. It's an easy answer, and it involves first doing something as objectively as we possibly can: we must accept ourselves, not conditionally, but completely. I've tried it and tested it out for myself. I am fully confident that you can do the same for yourself as well.

I remember when I used to be extremely hard on myself, going after my goals in life only to be disappointed when I achieved them, because the results were incongruent with what I had initially envisioned. Those goals of mine varied in type. Some of them involved making strides in getting things done in my corporate career. Others involved setting up my businesses and working with clients. Aside from those endeavors, I had other accomplishments to complete involving my home life and relationship goals. As I accomplished those things, I compared my accomplishments to those of others. I was getting what I wanted out of life, but I could never seem to attain happiness as I did that. Sure, I felt invigorated and energized as I accomplished my goals, but I did not achieve what I was truly after, *joy*. I wondered why this was the case. I could never seem to figure it out. I continued searching for answers outside of myself. I consulted with peers, mentors, and coworkers. I read self-help books, and I had lengthy conversations with my partner. I prayed as well. Oh, wow, how I prayed on this matter time and time again, always asking for answers, always waiting for them to come. So, as I accomplished, as I achieved, and as I gained, I also prayed and pined for happiness. Then, a shift in my thinking began to occur. As I collected feedback on my efforts and accomplishments while piecing together what I was doing and what it all meant to me, I noticed that I was calling out to myself, not just to others and God. The person who was failing to define who he was and what he stood for in life was *me*. And there were a whole lot of answers I had not provided to myself as I built the very brands that were pouring out of me for myself and my businesses. Now, that truly was an ah-hah moment for me!

> **"I WAS BETTER ABLE TO CARE ABOUT WHAT OTHERS THOUGHT ABOUT ME AND MY BUSINESSES ONLY AFTER I STARTED CARING FOR AND HONORING MYSELF MOST OF ALL."**

I became fully open to accepting, assessing, and objectively responding to what others thought of me, my personal brand, and my business branding efforts only after I fully accepted myself. I was better able to care about what others thought about me and my businesses only after I started caring for and honoring myself most of all. I think this is the key to learning how to permeate your branding efforts with your authenticity while paying attention to what others think of you. Sure, I do agree with people when they say, "You should not care about what others think of you." But I only agree given certain context around that statement. People should not care about what others think of them as a sole guide for living. People's thoughts about us should not dictate our actions. If they do, that means we are living our lives, performing our activities, and running our businesses for everyone else except ourselves. This is one of the surest paths to living a life of misery. So instead, I urge others to learn more about themselves, love themselves, and know themselves, deeply, inside and out before considering any feedback they get from others. Only then, can you compare what others think of you and how the market has been responding to you based on a true baseline. That baseline is your deliberate and undeniable truth.

It's a Spiritual Thing.

How do you get to know yourself? Today, I'm fortunate enough to truly know myself. I'm happy to have finally become extremely clear on who I am, what I want to do, what I will and will not accept, and what matters most for me in life and in business. But that was not an easy journey for me. I've had struggles in the past with many of the things I now help my clients with. At one point in my life, I was extremely unclear about what I wanted to do or was supposed to be doing. As I engaged in various ventures, I found myself going in many different directions, struggling to focus. I was sometimes going in circles as well. I experienced misery in moments when my lack of clarity overwhelmed me. I would become sad and couldn't quite pin down what was causing that sadness. But again, I believe those moments of sadness were caused by my lack of focus coupled with me not fully knowing myself.

One day, I decided to make a change and dig deeper within myself to figure out what was going on with me and my disappointments. I centered my thoughts on the realization that I am more than just a physical body. I dwelled on the fact that I am the embodiment of energy and a life force that gives meaning to everything else around me. And as I did that, I entered still moments of prayer whereas I asked God for guidance for finding my way. I asked God for clarity of thought and actions in my life, my work, and my brand. At this point, you may wonder how I thought to pray for my branding efforts. People don't often mention praying about establishing a successful personal or business brand. But for me, I must mention this within the pages of this book. I prayed for having beautiful brands for both my business and personal ventures because I profoundly understood the connection between branding and life events. Because I had worked in the creative field of marketing and graphics design, I could see how some components of branding I built with my clients were already helping them. I know my prayers worked. Today, I feel more complete in my life than I ever have before. I go about my daily routines with ease knowing I am branding myself and my efforts just as I should be. Yet, praying by itself did not make me feel that way. Prayer is what burst the dam and let the waters flow regarding an understanding that I must intertwine my DNA and spirit with everything I brand.

Living your life with deliberate intentions is thoroughly rewarding, and branding does not exist outside the scope of this. That connection was a powerful one for me to make. If I had to provide you a visual of what occurred in my mind once I figured that out, I would say it was as if there had been swirling clouds and thunderstorms around me. Those clouds all of a sudden diminished to give way to sunny blue skies. A profound state of clarity came over me. That clarity remains with me to this very day. And although I never knew it would be possible back then, I now know that clarity and focus continues to get better over time. Clarity and focus evolves with you. Thus, when you couple them with your personal and business branding efforts, your brands evolve as well. It's truly a beautiful thing!

Your brand can be viewed and understood as an entirely different entity than yourself. And phenomenally, your DNA is woven into it. Another viewpoint is that your brand has a soul. That soul is the conglomeration of various pieceparts of your own soul that you decided to mix in. What's fantastic about this phenomenon is that other human beings will respond to your brand, whether it's a personal brand or a business brand. It's inevitable. That's something you should consider to be immensely powerful. Even weightier is the fact that you have complete control of it, should you choose to acknowledge that fact or not. So, why not be intentional with your branding? Nonetheless, please try to always remember, given our human limitations of bandwidth and capacity, brands are easier for people to process since they are summations of people and businesses. Brands shed the infinite details about people or businesses that onlookers would never be able to process. Think about

"LIVING YOUR LIFE WITH DELIBERATE INTENTION IS THOROUGHLY REWARDING, AND BRANDING DOES NOT EXIST OUTSIDE THE SCOPE OF THIS."

how quickly we'd all become overwhelmed in a world without brands. We should always keep this in mind when we think of branding for anything. A brand, whether it is a personal brand or a business brand, is the embodiment of characteristics and outcomes derived from your own creation. That's right, a little piece of you is embedded within every brand you own or help to create. Thus, you're never wrong when it comes to thinking about even the tiniest details regarding any of your branding efforts.

"WHEN WE INTENTIONALLY BREATHE LIFE INTO OUR BRANDS, THEY BECOME UNSTOPPABLE FORCES OF NATURE."

When we understand the spiritual component of branding, we learn how to wield our power with branding. When we intentionally breathe life into our brands, they become unstoppable forces of nature. If we fail to understand this, then we do harm to ourselves and our businesses. Think of it this way: given unclear or haphazard intentions, unclear or hazardous brands are born. If we are misguided or deceitful during our branding efforts, we create misguided or deceitful brands. Irrevocably, the fruits of your labor, or your brand "children" will reflect poorly on you as a result. The main point I'm making here is that creating great brands requires soul searching. After performing this fundamental activity, you will be able to ensure the best parts of you and your best intentions are integrated with your brand's DNA. Thus, if you are truly seeking to make soul connections with those you reach, you must be cognizant of the fact that as you fold in your intentions, your soul-searching efforts will pay off thanks to the *Law of Attraction*. What a great lead-in for the next section of this book!

What should you do after reading this section?

1. *Identify some criticism you have received regarding your personal or your business brand. Acknowledge how you felt about that criticism. Be clear with yourself regarding whether or not you became annoyed or angered by that criticism. Make an attempt to treat that criticism as constructive feedback.*

2. *If you are currently branding yourself or your business, and you are receiving feedback and responding to it, determine if you are becoming overwhelmed doing so. If you are becoming overwhelmed, think about how you might use your own voice and desires to cut through all those divergent feedback channels.*

3. *If you have begun focusing on your branding*

efforts, identify areas that you have sought to embed pieces of your soul or DNA within. If you cannot identify any, then derive a list of your personal characteristics to be embedded in your branding efforts.

— V. YOUR BRAND AND THE LAW OF ATTRACTION . . . THAT'S PLAYING WITH FIRE.

The Highlights of This Section You Should Know:

- ***You will come to know that branding corresponds to the Law of Attraction. Your branding efforts create impressions on and reactions from everyone who experiences them.***

- ***You will know that the Law of Attraction will bring to you what you desire based on your thoughts and feelings. However, your thoughts and feelings may not be in alignment with what you say you desire.***

- ***You will learn that you can detrimentally impact your branding efforts by looking outside of yourself to define them. You will become aware***

that you can build unhappiness into your branding efforts by starting from a mental state of unhappiness and emptiness.

- ***You will learn that branding can be established to market your truth as it relates to your personal brand or your business brand. It can also be established to help gain validation by others in the marketplace. You will understand the consequences of both options.***

Even though people don't intuitively think about the point I'm about to bring up now, I'm going to lay it out for you. For me, this is something very clear in my mind. I hope to make it very clear in your mind as well. Here goes: branding is very powerful and spiritual, and it directly correlates to the Law of Attraction. I have personally come to realize, experience, accept, and utilize it as a means to navigate my life's journey, even right now. So, how are branding and the Law of Attraction related? Well, on the bright side, when you brand yourself or a business, you actually create ways to draw people to you and change how the world responds to you and your business. Better yet, you also create ways to repel people and some events in the world that could be damaging to your life's mission.

Yet, just because the Law of Attraction can positively affect your life by drawing outcomes unto you per your desires, that does not mean you will always get what you think you desire. If your thoughts are not in sync with your emotions regarding what you desire, you will more than likely attract to yourself what you feel strongest about. If you are more concerned or apprehensive about a negative occurrence in your life while you keep telling yourself great things will happen, it is likely you'll attract more hardships than success. That's because the Law of Attraction teaches us that we attract to ourselves what our minds and emotions focus on the most. Both the conscious and subconscious minds play a part within us all. You could be consciously telling yourself you will succeed while your subconscious mind nags at you about impending failures. Your struggle might be a tug of war between your conscious and subconscious minds. The part of your consciousness that is attached to your strongest feelings will draw to you the outcomes it is focused on the most. Those outcomes could be positive, or they could be negative.

"IF YOUR THOUGHTS ARE NOT IN SYNC WITH YOUR EMOTIONS REGARDING WHAT YOU DESIRE, YOU WILL MORE THAN LIKELY ATTRACT TO YOURSELF WHAT YOU FEEL STRONGEST ABOUT."

Remember, branding provides us an opportunity to attract outcomes that align with our life and business goals. It's always working with us. *And it is always fair*. If provided the opportunity, it will function as a means to bring to us reflections of all the negativity we might harbor inside. So, as we operate within the guardrails of the Law of Attraction, and as we build into our brands various components based on our shortcomings and fears, we quite possibly could attract to us the very things that poke at our fears and insecurities. If negative thoughts are what we choose to focus on, then our resultant brands will exist to fight fears and come to blows with roadblocks that make us insecure. Isn't that what the brand will have been developed to do? What will happen is that fears and roadblocks will always show up for us to put our brands to the test and fight for us. And we'll constantly need to operate in a defensive state. This type of incorrect branding is something that can bring upon you negative outcomes you did not adequately anticipate. It will then beg

"THERE IS EITHER BRANDING THAT WORKS FOR YOU, AND BRANDING THAT DOES NOT. THAT'S COMPLETELY UP TO YOU."

the question, "Where did I go wrong?" So, what exactly is *incorrect branding*?

Optimistically speaking, I believe there is really no such thing as incorrect branding. There is either branding that works for you, and branding that does not. That's completely up to you. You get to choose what you want to happen in your life. However, you must be proactive, not haphazard about it. The Law of Attraction is a tool you can use to ensure you develop branding practices for yourself that work in accordance with your inner desires, thoughts, and feelings. If you are not familiar with the Law of Attraction, my suggestion for you is to quickly get your hands on a copy of or listen to the audiobook for *The Law of Attraction: The Basics of the Teachings of Abraham* by Esther and Jerry Hicks. This book is a fantastic, life-changing read. It describes the Law of Attraction in details you may never have heard before. I cannot do you any justice here in my writing to get you to fully understand it and use it for your own gains. But the main takeaway you should know is that the Law of Attraction not only responds to your thoughts but also your genuine feelings and emotions. Emotions combined with thoughts trigger how God and the Universe interact with you. For this very reason, I once again urge you to be very authentic with your desires for branding.

Do you believe your thoughts for branding reflect your truth as you read these pages? Are you seeking to develop your personal or business brand because it will embody your authentic, universal purpose? Rather, are you seeking to develop a brand for yourself or your business that reflects the world validating you as you overcome your own internal issues and insecurities? Believe me, you will get exactly what your heart latches onto. You may not be able to articulate what's in your mind and in your heart, but remember, branding is a spiritual thing. You can feel it. God and the Universe need no words to respond to the essence of your truth. Allow me to unpack this for you.

> **"OPTIMISTICALLY SPEAKING, I BELIEVE THERE IS REALLY NO SUCH THING AS INCORRECT BRANDING. THERE IS EITHER BRANDING THAT WORKS FOR YOU, AND BRANDING THAT DOES NOT."**

There is a great deal of unhappiness in the world today. In fact, I will venture to say the economy thrives on society's general sentiment that at our cores, we all struggle to believe we are good enough. The very thing that drives sales in today's economy are notions that we need everything everyone else is trying to sell us. For what we don't have, the average advertisement attempts to convince us we won't be okay unless we have those missing products and services in our lives. So, there is a bit of emptiness inside each and every one of us that others are counting on. They want to take advantage of that. If you don't find yourself, you will be swept away by the tides of everyday, tumultuous society. If you do not fill up that void of unhappiness inside yourself, then something else will fill it up for you. The questions I posed previously about the purpose of your branding efforts play right into this fact. Do you believe your thoughts for branding reflect your truth? Or are you seeking to develop a brand for the validation of others? As you go about your daily life, are you seeking to evolve while operating from a place of emptiness or not?

Think of yourself as a shopper in a marketplace somewhere. What's on the shopping list for today? Let's imagine you're going shopping for the components of your brand. In the place you're going, there are a lot of stores to choose from. Everybody has a storefront there, *including you*. But some stores are larger than others. Some of them are huge! They have much more presence and influence. Regardless, every store has items you can use for your brand.

So, what store will you start with? Will you choose your store or the store of someone else to obtain components for your brand? The choice will be difficult. All of those stores will vye for your attention. They will all be able to assist you. But all of them will not benefit you in the same way. In fact, they will be vying for your attention so much, they will attempt to distract you from what you really need. Most of them will not really care about what you require. Instead, they will primarily care about getting your attention and selling to you. They won't care about your presence and influence. They will focus on keeping their rank and influence intact while attempting to capture your attention. Sure, what you buy from them will benefit you in some way. What you purchase from them may make you happy as well, for a while. But how far will that happiness go? By selling to you, those other stores will be extending their reach via the branding components they sell to you. But the items in your store that you overlooked will stay right there, untapped and unused. Be aware of this. Be careful. Most importantly, don't sell yourself short.

Think of the shopping basket you were filling with all the brand components to alleviate the void within you and your branding efforts. You could have either started filling that shopping basket with stuff other people were selling or with items you already had in your inventory. The most important

"MOST PEOPLE JUST CAN'T SEE BEYOND THEIR OWN CURRENT CIRCUMSTANCES, SO THEY ONLY BELIEVE THEY ARE CAPABLE OF DOING WHAT THEY HAVE ALREADY SEEN OTHERS DO."

thing to know here is that where you start shopping absolutely matters. Only one of those stores in the entire shopping complex has items in it that you can purchase and also tailor or reinvent per your own particularities. *It's yours*. Sadly, based on my own experiences dealing with my clients over the years, I know that many people, if not most, do not start filling their shopping carts with items from their own branding inventories. That is because they have been conditioned by society to think of themselves as sheep in a field shepherded by other brands. They have been trained by society to default to a place of emptiness by which to live. Most people just can't see beyond their own current circumstances, so they only believe they are capable of doing what they have already seen others do. Branding is no exception. In that big shopping complex of branding, they will choose to overlook selections from their own inventories because they just don't like or don't value what they have to offer. They are *unhappy* with their offerings. The world has conditioned them to think this way. They believe someone else or something else has offerings to make them happy regarding the brands they seek to create. Wow! How unfortunate is that? To make matters worse, they will mimic things that just won't resonate or be authentic for them in the realm of branding. They will overlook something very important. They will disregard just how valuable their inventories already are for what's in their current toolbelt to build their brands. They will fill up that unhappy void they have inside with unnecessary or distracting stuff, items that are out of alignment with their essence for building their personal and business brands. Thus, their brands will eventually "fail" simply because the foundation was insufficient at the very start. The fundamental truth is that if you are not careful, your new start with branding may be grounded in unhappiness because you unintentionally set it up that way. You may not have meant to do so. Still, my most candid advice to you is to try to avoid this as much as you possibly can. It will only slow you down.

If your thoughts are centered around finding your truth to reflect that in your branding efforts, then find hope in knowing it will come. That is the best way to fill the void you might now have for personal or business branding. Avoid the distractions. Sure, learn from others, but listen to your mind and your heart first. Enhance your branding efforts only with the lessons learned from others. Do not let thoughts of deficiency settle in for you. When it comes to branding, one of the best things you can possibly do for yourself is go against the grain. Still, always be very intentional with your actions. Always keep in mind that finding your own joy, not trying to capture the joy of others in your efforts, is the key for both branding . . . and living a great life in general!

In your efforts to find your joy in branding, be fully confident in knowing that same joy will eventually permeate your brand. I call that *branding on purpose*. In fact, I have a coaching focus entitled **Branding on Purpose** as part of my Plurapreneur® coaching practice. **Branding on Purpose** is purely intentional. The end goal for this activity is the establishment of a reciprocal outcome whereas the same joy you bring to others will come right back to you. You'll simply attract it. You will also gain profound clarity for your life, your brand, and your overall participation in life. By branding on purpose with the intentions I'm laying out for you in this book, you will be filling up your void, or your shopping basket for branding, with knowledge of your own self worth. If you don't start with yourself, you will always end up attempting to model yourself after what you see in the world and in others. You will always be chasing the validation of others, thereby reinforcing negative thought patterns around never feeling you are good enough. For both life and business, you'll be setting up a brand that exudes insecurity and a general sense of lacking for everyone else to see, observe, assess, and respond to. Success for you will always be a moving target as well. You'll never understand what defines the joy you seek, because you will be too focused on gathering inputs from others, rather than composing the definition of it for yourself. How will you ever find happiness by sifting through all those thoughts and opinions? Chaos will attract chaos. Unhappiness will attract even more unhappiness. You will also attract a whole bunch of the wrong attention and even more people in your life who will do little to nothing to enhance your life.

> **"SURE, LEARN FROM OTHERS, BUT LISTEN TO YOUR MIND AND YOUR HEART FIRST. DO NOT LET THOUGHTS OF DEFICIENCY SETTLE IN FOR YOU."**

The Law of Attraction isn't like a light switch. You can't simply turn it on at some point in the future, based on your convenience. No. It is, in fact, responding to you and working for or against you at this very moment. As time goes on, it will continue to do the very same thing. You will either continue to ignore it or work with it. So there is no more important moment than now to adjust the trajectory of your life for the roads you want to travel regarding your branding activities. If you're insistent on taking control of your brand now, then stop filling up that empty or unhappy void with external, inauthentic junk.

Do you want to develop a brand for yourself that genuinely radiates from your mind, body, and soul? If the answer is yes, and you truly set your intentions on this, then something fantastic will begin to happen for you. You will start moving about in the world differently as you plan your next steps. You will perhaps take note of what has been working for you and what has not been working as you recognize what it really takes to brand yourself or your business. You will define your mission, your purpose, and your objectives. You will ensure they all intertwine and capture your genuine interests. You will not consider at this point what others think you should do, or what others have been doing that you think you should do as well. No, instead, you will finally take time out for yourself to get to know who you are, why you exist, and what you should be doing that drives your zest for life. Then, you will be finally clear, firmly rooted in who you. You will be able to truly pour yourself and your essence into living your life per your will. And you will do so completely based on your own terms. However, keep in mind that existing and running a business can't be done in a vacuum. You will still need to gain peers, customers, and clients who will support you in your efforts. That is more hard work you'll do and complete as you successfully reach your goals. What's comforting about getting clear with yourself before branding yourself and your business is that you will have an established and succinct baseline. You will become rooted in your unique purpose. And as you continue to grow and develop throughout

"IF YOU'RE INSISTENT ON TAKING CONTROL OF YOUR BRAND NOW, THEN STOP FILLING UP THAT EMPTY OR UNHAPPY VOID WITH EXTERNAL, INAUTHENTIC JUNK."

your efforts, you will be better prepared to pivot, scale, and expand while not losing yourself in the process.

Do you want to develop a brand that validates who you are? Do you want to see the admiration in the eyes of others as you evolve as a person, lead an effort, or build a business that thrives? If your answer is yes, then you will study how others respond to you. You will figure out what you can do to garner praise and support from others. Every action you take will reflect a call to action for others to respond to you. And you will get results. However, it's important to know that with this decision comes the forfeiture or demotion of the pursuit to understand yourself and put your unique purposes and desires above those of others. And in the process of branding yourself, you will come to realize that you will attract not only the ability to receive validation of your successful branding, but also the criticism of others who will inadvertently help you realize you are putting off dealing with your own personal issues. Our ideal state is to exist whereas we create a life for ourselves that makes us happy . . . not superficially happy, but *authentically* happy. Moving through the world performing actions that get the results we desire devoid of our intentions to meet our authentic needs and desires only enables a singular, unavoidable outcome. The world will force you to recognize that you are delaying what should matter most to you: you must seek to understand exactly who you are in this world so that you can evolve while finding happiness and joy in life. You are the only person who can do that for yourself.

The Law of Attraction is indeed very powerful, but it's only one of the great laws of the Universe. There are several more. My intent with this book is not to provide you with lessons on what those laws are. Instead, I will recommend another book to you called *The Kybalion: A Study of the Hermetic Philosophy of Ancient Egypt and Greece* by the Three Initiates. For the purposes of this book, I will only bring to your attention another great principle of existence called the Law of Polarity. This principle embodies the universal truth that everything exists in the form of polar opposites. Simply put, within the context of this book on branding, you can never experience good things without experiencing some bad things as well. You can never have it easy without encountering something difficult. Branding yourself and your business is no exception. And the Law of Attraction works in tandem with the Law of Polarity. In fact, they somewhat conspire to make you a better person in your evolutionary journey. As I mentioned previously in this chapter of my book, if you seek to create an authentic brand that resonates with who you are at the core, you will still have to do the hard work of figuring out how your unique purposes and gifts align with working with others. You will have to eventually be flexible and negotiate what parts of your branding remain pure and what others are tailored to meet your personal and business goals. If you are seeking to create a brand that directly addresses what people and the marketplace want from you, you will eventually have to come to terms with how much of yourself you must compromise, or even sacrifice, to get the results you want. Oh yes, you will never get off easy when it comes to branding. But if you know what you must consider on the front end of establishing that "best brand" for you or your business, what's to come will not be roadblocks for you, but rather challenges you must understand, learn to navigate, and move beyond.

What should you do after reading this section?

1. *Determine what you consider to be incorrect branding activities you are currently performing. Determine the reason why you consider those branding efforts to be incorrect.*

2. *Identify what your motivation for branding is right now. Be clear with yourself enough to know whether you are seeking promotion of your truth in your brand or seeking validation of your brand by others.*

3. *Recognize what brings you joy in your branding efforts. Identify plans to build on that joy and make it sustainable for attracting more of that joy in the future.*

4. *Commit to learning more about the Law of*

Attraction. My suggestion for you is to read the hard copy or listen to the audio book of "The Law of Attraction: The Basics of the Teachings of Abraham" by Esther and Jerry Hicks."

— VI. WHEN BRANDING FAILS FOR YOU, DO THIS.

The Highlights of This Section You Should Know:

- ***You will understand that branding can be frustrating and difficult. You can embrace the complexity of branding by letting go of your expectations that there is a specific way to brand yourself or your business. Instead, you will realize you must clearly demand your desires for branding, and work on implementing your unique branding requirements.***

- ***You will gain an appreciation for carving out your own path for branding yourself or your business rather than mimicking what you see other people or businesses do.***

- ***You will further gain an appreciation for your branding failures. Whether you succeed or fail***

in meeting your branding expectations, you are able to learn a lesson from every challenge you face.

- ***You will acknowledge that you can experiment with your branding efforts; however, experimenting may not be efficient.***

There is no perfect way to brand yourself or your business. There is definitely not a one size fits all solution for branding of any kind. For this reason, branding can be one of the most challenging and disappointing activities to execute. Generally speaking, people tend to think that branding consists of specific actions that should be done to guarantee success. To some extent, that is true; however, for the most part, branding has a component of uncertainty that is completely unpredictable. That uncertainty is what causes people to sometimes think they are failures when it comes to branding. They might plan for things to go a certain way as a result of their branding efforts, and the outcomes might play out in a completely different way than what was expected. Something that many people don't think about when this happens is the fact that those plans may have been derived from unrealistic expectations at the very start.

Branding is demanding. It requires you to be very specific and realistic regarding what you require of it. You cannot expect your brand to function well for you if you are looking for a miracle worker. Your brand cannot work miracles for you if you cannot work miracles for yourself. Remember, your brand is an embodiment of you, packaged to attract certain outcomes in your life. Even if you don't think you're asking for miracles to be performed, you may be looking for small unrealistic wins. For example, a common expectation that people have regarding branding is that their actions will result in outcomes for them just like other people's branding activities have resulted for them. Just because you are doing what someone else is doing, I can assert that you will not be guaranteed the same outcomes. Just because you use the same words, wear the same clothes, and attempt to look like someone else, that does not mean you will live the same life they do or run the same types of businesses they do. Isn't that

> **"BRANDING IS DEMANDING. IT REQUIRES YOU TO BE VERY SPECIFIC AND REALISTIC REGARDING WHAT YOU REQUIRE OF IT. YOU CANNOT EXPECT YOUR BRAND TO FUNCTION WELL FOR YOU IF YOU ARE LOOKING FOR A MIRACLE WORKER."**

asking for a miracle? Isn't that like asking God to give you the same life someone else has? Perhaps God would frown upon this. We are all unique on purpose. We have individual gifts that I believe God has bestowed upon us to individually build and evolve the collective human experience. Thus, the Universe enables us to embrace this job of ours and excel. However, because many of us do not cherish our own gifts as much as we possibly could, we fail at branding . . . and perhaps a host of other things in our lives.

So, what do you do when your personal brand or your business brand fails? Again, I believe failure isn't really failure. At the very least, failure is subjective for all of us. What does failure mean for you? You must start there. In order to know what failure means for you, you must clearly know what success means for you too. Please keep in mind that "for you" are the operative words in that statement. We often start out traveling the wrong paths for branding ourselves and our businesses by looking for easy springboards and quick starts to get our brands off the ground. When we do that, we tend to lack a primary voice in our efforts. That voice is our own. Instead, we use someone else's blueprint for branding success. Then, when our brands "fail," we wonder why. The reason is that, in those moments, we entangle ourselves in trying to figure out someone else's problem. How so, you ask?

Well, the fact is that we think we're looking for the answers for our failed branding attempts when we're actually wondering why someone else's brand didn't work for us. We cheated ourselves.

Have you ever engaged in branding activities by mimicking someone else? How did that work out for you? Did you get the results you were looking for? Or did you "fail" at branding regardless of how hard you tried? You more than likely fell short in creating that branding success you saw for the person you mimicked. Still, I'm here to assure you that all is not lost. How can you fail at something you never really understood or resonated with in the first place? Trying on someone else's brand is like running an experiment on yourself. It's as if you are conducting a test, using all the same variables for two completely different test specimens. Your life experiences are different from that of any other person in this world. You look different. You act and execute differently. And you have infinitely many more unique characteristics that are incongruent with the branding activities you were mimicking. Thus, in the end, all you really did was test how some disparate branding activities worked for your unique circumstances. Isn't that enlightening? Now, you should realize that this experiment was destined to yield different results for you. You did not code any of your DNA, spirit, and heart into those branding activities, or "experiments," you performed. And, sadly, you wasted valuable time, skipping over the essential step of learning who you are at your core. That is what was needed to be packaged for your personal or your business brand.

Most people and businesses that succeed at branding are those that have settled on clear and realistic goals for themselves. And as time went on, they intertwined those life or business goals with their branding activities. Another way of thinking of this is that those successful brands had people behind them who clearly defined their success criteria and planned for strategic branding execution. That success criteria was clearly defined, and their unique desires in life or business were included. Successful brands rarely copy other brands. Instead they *learn* from other brands. Sure, they may lift branding processes from other successful brands. However, they work very hard to bring to the forefront that one-of-a-kind perspective that makes them different from any other brand in the marketplace. That is what becomes their competitive edge in branding and marketing themselves.

When branding "fails," there is only one thing to do. You must go back to the drawing board. If you believe your personal branding or your business branding activities are failing, then try to first understand your initial intentions. If you "failed" at branding yourself or your business, think about what led to those failures. Did you start as you should have, by baselining who you are now or what your business currently is and does? That baseline is what will provide you with the north star pointing you toward the future of your personal or business branding success. Did you map specific branding activities to various specific outcomes you desire? Were the outcomes you defined realistic? Did the success criteria you defined for yourself come from within? Were they authentic or did you completely base your success criteria on what you noticed someone else or some other business experiencing? These are key questions you should use to drive yourself toward the answers for your failed attempts at branding. You must understand the "why" before moving on to the "what" you should do next.

"MOST PEOPLE AND BUSINESSES THAT SUCCEED AT BRANDING ARE THOSE THAT HAVE SETTLED ON CLEAR AND REALISTIC GOALS FOR THEMSELVES."

Failure should be fully recognized as something you acknowledge based on your own pure will and volition. Never use anyone else's criticism or requirements for success as your sole basis for success. Only you hold the answers for knowing what works best for you. Only you can create the authentic success and happiness that means the most for you. For me, failure became the identification of not accomplishing something for myself that I deemed necessary for achieving my joy. At one time in my life, I associated my successful branding with how other people branded themselves or their businesses. However, as I did the work to grow and evolve myself, I soon developed something very profound: a powerful inclination to finally listen to my inner voice, devoid of distractions. That inner voice urged me to latch onto what was different and special about me. I began doing the work to evolve beyond what society and people around me deemed

"FAILURE SHOULD BE FULLY RECOGNIZED AS SOMETHING YOU ACKNOWLEDGE BASED ON YOUR OWN PURE WILL AND VOLITION. NEVER USE ANYONE ELSE'S CRITICISM OR REQUIREMENTS FOR SUCCESS AS YOUR SOLE BASIS FOR SUCCESS."

as criteria for success. Only then, did I begin to experience branding success that was joyous for me.

What should you do after reading this section?

1. *Decide to continue refining or evolving your branding efforts versus completely starting over with your branding efforts. Decide what makes sense for you based on what you consider to be your branding failures. It's all a matter of perspective and what you "feel" is best for you.*

2. *Determine whether or not you are specific with your branding expectations in accordance with your unique circumstances? If you are, ensure you have success criteria for your personal branding or business branding that is realistically and clearly defined as well.*

— VII. BRANDING COMES FIRST BECAUSE IT IS PERSONAL.

The Highlights of This Section You Should Know:

- ***You will be encouraged to prioritize branding for yourself or your business as a primary, proactive activity that improves your life.***

- ***You will be provided insights from me regarding how the lack of prioritizing intentional branding led to a stressful health condition and some internal emotional conflicts.***

I cannot stress to you just how important branding is for any successful person or business. So, even though lots of people still think of branding activities as secondary chores they do to improve their lives or create their businesses, I tend to help them think of branding as a primary concern. As you've read the pages of this book, I hope you have gained some compelling insights regarding just how powerful your brand can be. I hope you see your brand as a powerful tool, or even a helpful "friend," that can help you create limitless potential and thus reach phenomenal goals.

Branding should always be a forethought. However, most of us consider branding for ourselves or our businesses to be an afterthought. We might run off into the world chasing our careers or toiling to build our businesses when after days, weeks, or even years have passed, we finally think about solid, strategic branding. Hindsight is 20/20. By that time, we come to realize we should have been thinking about branding much earlier. Branding is something that is done to help you get what you want out of life and business. A branding strategy is something that is developed to guide our actions in alignment with how we view ourselves and our businesses in the world. In conjunction with that, we should also use our branding methods to influence how others perceive us and our businesses, as we see fit.

> **"BRANDING IS SOMETHING THAT IS DONE TO HELP YOU GET WHAT YOU WANT OUT OF LIFE AND BUSINESS."**

Branding can be used for good or evil, and everything else in between. However, I believe we as human beings prefer to travel the paths of least resistance. For me–and I think as is the case for most others–the path of least resistance in life is the one you travel that aligns with who you are at the core. That's the good and happy path. It's also the path that usually involves less work. We will still have to engage in hard work; however, that work will be less taxing on our minds and spirits. That's the beauty of living with integrity, operating from a place of light and goodness. Conversely, living based on lies and beguiled trickeries takes more of an effort than living in truth. Undoubtedly, it will take a lot more work for us to bamboozle and cheat our ways through successful branding efforts. Truth always prevails in the wake of lies that must always be patched up with even more lies that follow. For that exact reason, we should always consider how we engage in branding as we venture into living better lives and leading new successful businesses. If we do not, then we run the risk of making a slew of poor decisions. Dire outcomes will need to be rectified when we finally figure out how our brands should be positioned for wholesome, good-natured, and joyful success.

When you begin any new journey in life, why not think about how it aligns with your essence at the very start? Being clear with yourself and level setting everyone else around you is of utmost importance. It's precisely what you must do if you want all the pieces of your life experiences and business dealings to fall into place harmoniously. The hardest decisions you will ever make are the ones that involve you deciding what you must do to stand out. However, you must always be truthful with what you identify as your unique characteristics for your

"THE HARDEST DECISIONS YOU WILL EVER MAKE ARE THE ONES THAT INVOLVE YOU DECIDING WHAT YOU MUST DO TO STAND OUT."

branding efforts. It's just a matter of taking pride in your own particularities opposed to wanting those of others featured in your branding methods. That will always make a world of a difference for you. Sure, everyone learns the basics for getting a job, landing a great career, starting a new business, and running day to day operations. But if you're not clear with yourself regarding how much of that really resonates with you, you'll end up doing wonderful things that you despise. One of the worst feelings you can have is excelling at a job or a business that you hate. Take it from me, it feels awful. And I have experienced disappointments within both the corporate as well as the freelance environments regarding succeeding at efforts that did not resonate with my essence. In other words, I succeeded at efforts that were out of alignment with my purposeful existence.

In the corporate world, I remember a time when I rarely offered the answer of "no" for taking on any project or challenge. That was during my early career development years. As I think back on those moments, I clearly see how my lack of confidence influenced every decision I made. I was only focused on showing and proving my worth to my leaders and my peers. I did the exact opposite of what I do today, which is take into account the opportunities that lay in front of me, and then decide on participating in the ones that resonate with my unique aspirations. Back then, however, I questioned my abilities, despite the fact that I was indeed hired based on my education and expertise. Still, as I wondered how I was perceived in the eyes of others, I developed a persona in my workplace that attracted high stress and intense environments. As I excelled, I also began to dislike my work. I started to realize that I could no longer find happiness in my work because I was too busy trying to be a perfectionist and fix the problems of others. But what about my problems? Before I knew it, years had passed, and I had not prioritized my happiness as it related to me finding satisfaction in my work. I was instead going through the motions of being attentive to the needs of others, and deprioritizing my needs. I wanted to be viewed as a valuable employee at my workplace, and that's all that mattered. Eventually, all of that focusing on my job and downplaying my needs caught up with me. I was forced to learn that life is balanced. Oh, how much so I know that now! I abruptly realized that if you focus too much on one thing in your life, then something else will suffer in return. I began to experience migraine headaches due to the amount of stress I allowed to stockpile on me over the years. Then, something worse happened. I began to experience flashes in my right eye. It most often occurred when I sat at my desk at work looking into the computer monitor. At first, I paid little attention to it. But eventually, I Googled what that symptom may be indicative of. I came across several ailments, but the two that especially caught my attention were posterior vitreous detachment and retinal detachment. That's when I knew something serious was happening to me. As I dug deeper into what was happening with my health, I learned that I may have been suffering from a condition called central serous retinopathy. It's a medical condition in which fluid accumulates under the retina, causing a serous detachment and vision loss. I also experienced some pain in the back of my eye socket. And yes, stress is a major contributor to the development of the condition. I was literally losing my vision in one eye, and it was all because I was getting out of touch with caring for myself and my needs. After I was officially diagnosed with central serous retinopathy, and somewhat chastised by my eye doctor and ophthalmologist for not paying close attention to my health, I made a commitment to myself from then on to do better. I underwent a corrective procedure to stop the condition from progressing. However, I still receive those flashes in my right eye periodically. Thus, I continually monitor my stress levels and make time to find happiness in my life when I can. I feel much better in my life and in my career as a result. But I had to change my personal brand in the workplace to get to this point. Now, I have put better health practices in place for myself, given the fact I am much more focused on putting myself first and others second.

My experiences in my career have always mirrored some of my experiences in my freelance work. Just as I took on more stress than I should have in the workplace, so did I regarding my freelance work. Moving to a new city is always quite an adventure. When I moved from Louisiana to Texas, I was determined to make it a grand adventure whereas I would get acquainted with my new home while turning my creative hobbies into freelance work. I was already secure in my career, so that was all figured out. However, I have always considered having a side gig as a blanket of security I need to thrive. I went to work, explored the city, and partook in new and fun social activities. I also registered my new business with the City of Dallas and the Internal Revenue Service. Before I knew it, I had begun networking through new relationships I was creating. That old feeling of wanting to impress and please people began to settle in. Once again, it was laced with my own insecurities, and this time, I had no established reputation to pound my fist on. I was just settling into my new environment. I sought opportunities to work with people through my new creative services while the responses I received tugged at the value I brought to the table. People questioned my background, my motives, my skills, and even my worthiness to be acquainted with them. As I look back on those years, I see them quite differently as I did then. Back then, as I worked to become stronger, to navigate, and filter through all the challenging superficial social pathways and activities I endured to gain success, I grew out of touch with myself. I lost who I was at my core. Instead, I tried to be a people-pleaser. And because I was only in the preliminary stages of starting my freelance businesses in Dallas, I yielded to what people wanted from me, at all costs, instead of firmly establishing parameters around what was acceptable for me. In the case of establishing my freelance businesses, the stress I experienced was very different. Sure, it may have been a contributor to the central serous retinopathy ailment I acquired in my right eye. However, the stress I experienced throughout my freelance business affairs was more psychological. I experienced frustration and disappointment more than anything else. In those depressing moments of my dealings, unfortunately, I had not established my brand, or my "best friend." If I had, it could have yanked me out of those disappointing moments I struggled with. It could have helped me clearly communicate what was and what was not going to happen. It could have also helped me to demand, not tolerate, how I would put myself and my businesses out into the world.

As the years passed by, and as I learned, grew, excelled, performed, and became well-rooted in both my corporate career and my freelance business affairs, I must say that my life has certainly blossomed. The dust has settled. Everyday, clarity seems to unfold for me, and there are less unknowns to worry about. I can attribute a lot of that to my personal growth, my experience, and my willingness to learn more about life and who I am versus who I desire to be. Still, fused into those very outcomes are the fact that I had to become extremely clear with myself. I needed to define myself and offer that version of me to everyone else. In other words, I had to figure out my brand and my life within the constructs of my definitive acceptance. When that was done, I was better able to incorporate who I am into everything else I do. Undoubtedly, the reality that has followed me up to this very moment has aligned with what I need and desire. So what more is there for me to tell you about that? Well, I can tell you for sure that *I found joy*.

"THE DUST HAS SETTLED. EVERYDAY, CLARITY SEEMS TO UNFOLD FOR ME, AND THERE ARE LESS UNKNOWNS TO WORRY ABOUT."

What should you do after reading this section?

1. *Ask yourself if you are treating branding for you or your business as a primary activity in your life. If you are, then honor that commitment. Seek out ways you might improve your current branding activities. If you are not, then determine what you must do right now to make branding a primary focus in your life.*

2. *Determine whether or not branding is a stressful activity for you to perform. If it is, then make an effort to only focus on the activities that meet your true intentions. Release yourself from meeting other people's expectations or meeting someone else's standards for your branding efforts. Try to focus only on what you do best (what comes naturally for you).*

— VIII. PERSONALLY, THIS IS A BRAND NEW CONCLUSION.

The Highlights of This Section You Should Know:

- ***You will be reminded that although many, if not most, people know that branding is very important, they do not apply as much attention to it as they should.***

- ***You will be reminded that the lack of intentional branding leads to a world of confusion for improving yourself and building a business. The time to start is now.***

Do you have a brand?

"Well, if you don't think you have a personal brand, I'm here to tell you that you do. And if you're not controlling it, then someone else is."

Daymond The Brand, CLC

Once again, I'm reemphasizing this piece of advice for you. I teach a beginner's personal branding class called **Personal Branding 101**. I offer it to those branding clients and students of mine who desire to gain a basic understanding of what personal branding is. In the class, I also explain how it fits into their lives, and how they can begin branding themselves for authentic success. They even receive a set of worksheets to fill in with the starting points for the branding components they can work on. Obviously, I emphasize the recommendation that they should be intentional while doing so. From my own experiences, I can tell you that intentional branding is amazing. It has helped me tremendously. Because of good and solid branding practices, I have become very clear regarding who I am and how deliberate I am regarding everything I do. Because of branding, I now know how to articulate to others—for my own

> **"BRANDING IS SOMETHING EVERYONE KNOWS THEY NEED TO PAY ATTENTION TO. IRONICALLY, IT'S SOMETHING I WITNESS VERY FEW PEOPLE HANDLING WITH THE DELICACY AND ATTENTION THAT IT DESERVES."**

> **"BRANDING IS SOMETHING THAT REQUIRES YOU TO WORK ON YOURSELF. IT REQUIRES YOU TO FACE DIFFICULT CONCLUSIONS ABOUT YOURSELF, MANY OF WHICH YOU MAY NOT LIKE."**

advantage—what must be communicated, both in my personal and my business relationships. Because of branding, I know how to scope nearly every effort I take on, to thus maximize my capacity and joy, while minimizing regret and the build up of grudges. Because of personal branding, I now live in an undeniable truth fully integrated with purposeful living in accordance with my life's mission.

Branding is something everyone knows they need to pay attention to. Ironically, it's something I witness very few people handling with the delicacy and attention that it deserves. Yet, if they fully knew the happiness and joy it could bring to their lives, I know their actions would change. Honestly, I do not believe people desire to treat their branding activities as low priorities. I can validate this perception of mine by reminiscing about the many times I've had people tell me that they know they need to do more regarding their personal and business brands. What I think is the culprit for their procrastination is the fact that branding is very difficult. When I think about that difficulty, I don't only mean how intricate branding can be since it contains so many moving pieces. Branding is something that requires you to work on yourself. It requires you to face difficult conclusions about yourself, many of which you may not like. It's just easier to stay the same rather than force yourself to grow and evolve. Yet, that's exactly what branding helps you to do when you're ready. You just have to get over that first hurdle. Yes, you must get over yourself.

Becoming a brand new you involves having a very difficult conversation with yourself. You must figure out what it's going to take to get you to live up to your potential so that you can pour that into your life, your career, and your business. We all know that difficult conversations are things we often attempt to avoid, even when those conversations should be held with ourselves. As human beings, we are inherently risk averse. We will also avoid hard work at any cost sometimes. But taking on risks in life and performing hard work is exactly what makes you better and stronger.

The breaking point for me was that I finally got to a point in my life when I could no longer deal with the confusion I had regarding who I was. I had ideas about what the world expected of me; but somehow, all of that just felt wrong. Because I have such a staunch analytical mind, the fact that happiness never came from meeting those expectations that others had for me meant something was not right. Something was not computing. I had been cracking the code for meeting or exceeding my goals, but I was deceiving myself. I had been meeting goals that weren't my goals at all. Instead, they were goals others had for me. I had pulled them into my life as if they were my own. That's where I had gone wrong.

> "FOR ME, HARD WORK AND SELF-INTROSPECTION WAS MUCH NEEDED SO THAT I COULD BECOME AUTHENTICALLY ME."

Finally, I uncovered the power of personal branding for myself and my businesses. I knew it would be difficult to embark on that journey; however, I also knew it would be fulfilling. For me, hard work and self-introspection was much needed so that I could become authentically me. I accepted the fact that difficult times would come. The saving grace for me was my determination of getting past those difficult times to emerge as someone new, still me, but phenomenally stronger. And now, I take that version of me into every endeavor I pursue.

So, my question to you now, Evolver, is do you know that there is a brand new you out there somewhere? That brand new you is self-assured and determined to live in truth, unbothered by anyone else. That brand new you will show up at work everyday with no regrets, ready to take on any challenges and defeats, knowing each day is another opportunity to become victorious. That brand new you is ready to start a business or pour into an existing business, ready to mold that business into one that is unique, and ready to flourish in the grueling marketplace. That brand new you is strong and mighty, full of brawn. So, my last question for you, Evolver, is . . .

did you breathe life into that brand yet?

It's all up to you. XO.

What should you do after reading this section?

1. *Decide in this very moment the first steps you will take regarding taking control of your personal brand or your business brand. Attempt to define at least three efforts.*

2. *For those initial first steps you just defined in the step above, clearly define those steps as authentic and clear requirements that reflect your desires and your reality.*

3. *After you define your branding requirements, clearly define what success means for you meeting those branding requirements.*

4. *The next steps you take are action based. Plan the start dates and end dates for taking your next steps toward branding success. You got this!*

Sure.
Consistency may build character.
But authenticity fuels the soul.

— DAYMOND THE BRAND, CLC

— COPYRIGHT

THE BRAWN OF YOUR BRAND

Daymond & Co. Creative
2124 Farrington Street, Suite 350
Dallas, TX 75207

Daymond & Co. Creative is a subsidiary of
Daymond & Co. Enterprises, LLC, daymondco.com

Library of Congress Control Number: 2023904608

Hardcopy ISBN-13: 978-0-9961323-8-1

E-book ISBN-13: 978-0-9961323-7-4

Book Cover Design by Daymond E. Lavine,
Daymond E. Lavine, CLC of Daymond & Co. Creative, daymondcreative.com

10 9 8 7 6 5 4 3 2

For additional information about the author, to book a signing event, or for information on acquiring written permission in the case of brief quotations embodied in critical articles, interviews and reviews, visit www.DaymondCo.com.

This page is intentionally left blank.

This page is intentionally left blank.

www.ingramcontent.com/pod-product-compliance
Lightning Source LLC
Chambersburg PA
CBHW041917260326
41914CB00013B/1474

* 9 7 8 0 9 9 6 1 3 2 3 8 1 *